PARALLEL LIVES

HARVEY MILK

Born in 1930

DOLORES HUERTA

Julie Knutson

CHERRY LAKE PRESS

Published in the United States of America by Cherry Lake Publishing
Ann Arbor, Michigan
www.cherrylakepublishing.com

Reading Adviser: Marla Conn, MS, Ed., Literacy specialist, Read-Ability, Inc.
Cover Designer: Felicia Macheske

Photo Credits: © Courtesy of San Jose University Special Collections & Archives, cover, 1 [left]; © 1976 George Ballis/Take Stock/The Image Works, cover, 2 [right]; © Leonard Zhukovsky/Shutterstock.com, 5; © Library of Congress, LC-USF34-002462-E, 6; © Shawn Goldberg/Shutterstock.com, 9; © jubaphoto/iStock.com, 10; © Uncredited/AP/Shutterstock.com, 12; © ZUMA Press, Inc./Alamy Stock Photo, 15; © Glynnis Jones/Shutterstock.com, 16; © Everett Historical/Shutterstock.com, 19; © Arthur Schatz/Getty Images, 21; © David Talukdar/Shutterstock.com, 22; © mythja/Shutterstock.com, 24; © Library of Congress, LC-DIG-fsa-8b32536, 25; © Rena Schild/Shutterstock.com 26

Library of Congress Cataloging-in-Publication Data

Names: Knutson, Julie, author.
Title: Born in 1930 : Harvey Milk and Dolores Huerta / by Julie Knutson.
Other titles: Harvey Milk and Dolores Huerta
Description: Ann Arbor : Cherry Lake Publishing, [2020] | Series: Parallel lives | Includes index. | Audience: Grades 4-6
Identifiers: LCCN 2019033404 | ISBN 9781534159204 (hardcover) | ISBN 9781534161504 (paperback) | ISBN 9781534160354 (pdf) | ISBN 9781534162655 (ebook)
Subjects: LCSH: Social reformers—California—Biography—Juvenile literature. | Milk, Harvey—Juvenile literature. | Huerta, Dolores, 1930—Juvenile literature. | Mayors—California—San Francisco—Biography—Juvenile literature. | Gay politicians—California—San Francisco—Biography—Juvenile literature. | Gay men—California—San Francisco—Biography—Juvenile literature. | Women labor leaders—United States—Biography—Juvenile literature. | Mexican American women labor union members—Biography—Juvenile literature. | Mexican American migrant agricultural laborers—Labor unions—Organizing—History—Juvenile literature. | Gay liberation movement—California—San Francisco—History—20th century—Juvenile literature.
Classification: LCC F866.3 .K68 2020 | DDC 303.48/40922 [B]—dc23
LC record available at https://lccn.loc.gov/2019033404

Cherry Lake Publishing would like to acknowledge the work of the Partnership for 21st Century Learning, a Network of Battelle for Kids. Please visit www.battelleforkids.org/networks/p21 for more information.

Printed in the United States of America
Corporate Graphics

ABOUT THE AUTHOR

Julie Knutson shares a birth year with Venus Williams, Chelsea Clinton, and Lin-Manuel Miranda. An avid student of history and former teacher, she lives in northern Illinois with her husband and son.

TABLE OF CONTENTS

CHAPTER 1

Welcome to 1930

1930. American politician Harvey Milk and American labor leader Dolores Huerta are born into the world following the **stock** market crash of October 29, 1929. The crash sent the United States into the **Great Depression**, the worst economic downturn in its history. Lasting until 1939, the period was marked by widespread unemployment, homelessness, and hunger. As conditions worsened, certain groups of people were blamed for the country's declining fortunes. Dolores Huerta and Harvey Milk belonged to two of those groups. Throughout their lives, they witnessed the **stigma** associated with the groups to which they belonged.

The Stonewall riots were a response to a police raid on a known LGBT club in 1969.

LGBT Communities: When the economy collapsed in 1929, some blamed the "excessive" lifestyles of the 1920s. In the 1930s, moral codes sprung up, policing everything from what could be shown on movie screens to who could dance together in public places. These rules drove the **LGBT** community underground. Cities and states established laws forbidding people from wearing clothing of the opposite sex. In many places, restaurants and clubs would have their licenses to operate taken away if they served LGBT customers. And LGBT people faced very real threats to their well-being, ranging from job loss to arrests and beatings.

A majority of the Mexicans sent back to Mexico during the 1930s were American citizens by birth.

Mexican American/Latino Populations: In times of economic crisis, minority groups often find themselves under attack by politicians and the majority population. Mexicans and Mexican Americans who were welcomed as a labor source in the 1920s were suddenly blamed for taking jobs away from other Americans. Workers in agriculture, factories, and mines were fired by the thousands. Many government leaders encouraged **repatriation**. About one-third of Mexicans living in the United States were sent back to Mexico during this period.

What caused the Great Depression?

In the 1920s, a lot of Americans felt great about the economy. Many gambled on stocks, borrowed too much money from banks, or purchased too many goods on credit. None of these practices were sound or sustainable. They eventually led to the crash of 1929.

Harvey Milk
(b. May 22, 1930)

Like many activists, Harvey Milk firmly believed that "the personal is political." He thought that people shouldn't have to hide their identities and that all people have the right to live and love as they chose. Harvey was an openly gay man in a world that routinely denied LGBT rights. He encouraged others in the LGBT community to come out, use their voices, and demand full equality before the law. This was the cause for which he lived and died.

In 2015, same-sex marriage was legalized in the United States.

Homosexuality was listed as a mental disorder by the American Psychiatric Association until 1973.

Early Years: Finding a Voice

Harvey Milk was born in Woodmere, New York, on May 22, 1930. His family was active in the local business and Jewish communities. Harvey and his brother were mischievous kids with interests that ranged from movies to opera to football.

By his teen years, Harvey knew he was gay. But because of **homophobia**, he kept this a secret from family and friends. He worried about how his **sexual orientation** would affect his family, social life, and job prospects. So the secret stayed with him through college and into his 4-year military service with the U.S. Navy during the Korean War. He resigned from the Navy in 1955 and his secret continued to stay closely guarded throughout the 1950s and 1960s, when he taught high school and worked on **Wall Street**.

Paving the Way: Jose Sarria

Harvey Milk wasn't the first openly gay person to run for San Francisco's Board of Supervisors. In 1961, Jose Sarria ran for the same position. Sarria's early odds of winning one of the five open seats looked strong. But city officials who feared an LGBT supervisor recruited others to run against him. In the end, a total of 34 candidates appeared on the ballot. But the large field didn't stop Sarria. He campaigned in English and Spanish. His belief—"Equality Before the Law"—drew attention to civil rights issues and representation for gay voters. While he finished ninth in the 1961 contest, his openness and platform set the stage for future LGBT politicians.

Attendance at gay pride marches and parades grew in the 1970s.

It wasn't until Harvey moved to San Francisco, California, in the early 1970s that he openly shared that he was gay. Although San Francisco was home to a large LGBT population, **discrimination**, **harassment**, and violence were still widespread. Harvey owned a camera shop in the city's Castro District, and he decided to do something about it. He built community networks to support LGBT businesses. He held a street fair to draw people to the neighborhood. Soon, he became known as the "Mayor of Castro Street." He was speaking out and building support among many different groups of people, and preparing to run for office.

Middle Years: Expressing a Voice

Harvey believed that changing the law was necessary for creating lasting social impact, and it was this belief that drove him into politics. He ran in three elections—two for Board of Supervisors and one for State Assembly—before winning in 1977. With that win, he became one of the first openly LGBT politicians in the country and the first gay elected official in California's history. He took office as a city supervisor in 1978 and quickly got to work passing laws that recognized LGBT rights. In April 1978, San Francisco's mayor, George Moscone, signed an **ordinance** that made discrimination based on sexual orientation illegal. With all but one city supervisor supporting the measure, it was a huge victory.

But discrimination against the LGBT community didn't stop with the passing of that ordinance. "Proposition 6," a measure to ban gay and lesbian teachers from working in California, was on the ballot for November 1978. Harvey led the rallying cry against it. He debated the sponsor of the measure and educated the public about the proposal. He helped swing public opinion against the measure and celebrated its defeat on November 7, 1978.

Less than 3 weeks later, Harvey was **assassinated**. Dan White, the only supervisor to vote against the LGBT equality ordinance, shot him five times. The shocked city mourned the loss with a candlelight march from the Castro Street to City Hall. Between 25,000 and 40,000 people walked to remember Harvey.

White was tried for the murder. His lawyers argued that a combination of stress and junk food drove him to kill Harvey. He received a light sentence of 7 years in prison. The city erupted into riots and calls for justice.

In remembrance of his life, San Francisco residents have a candlelight march every year on the anniversary of Harvey's death.

Today, the rainbow flag is a global symbol of inclusion, pride, and hope.

Later Years: Leaving a Legacy

In life and in death, Harvey rallied millions of people to demand full recognition and equal opportunity for LGBT groups. His memory has been celebrated on everything from postage stamps to Navy ships, and he has been the subject of films and plays. In 1999, he was named one of *TIME* magazine's 100 most influential people of the 20th century. Today, the Harvey Milk Foundation continues his work, advocating globally for progress "not just for the LGBT community, but for all targets of hate, discrimination, and ignorance."

A Symbol of Pride

On June 25, 1978, the rainbow flag—a symbol of LGBT pride—made its first appearance at San Francisco's Gay and Lesbian Freedom Day Parade. Harvey Milk had worked with designer Gilbert Baker to create a symbol that would connect the community.

CHAPTER 3

Dolores Huerta
(b. April 10, 1930)

Over her 60-plus years as an activist, Dolores Clara Fernandez Huerta has inspired people around a range of issues. Best known for launching the farmworkers' movement alongside Cesar Chavez, Dolores made Americans think about the human side of food production. She tirelessly fought for fair wages, better working conditions, and access to education for agricultural laborers and their children.

During the Great Depression, shantytowns popped up across the country. These were poor communities with shacks constructed from cardboard boxes and other materials.

Early Years: Finding a Voice

Born in New Mexico on April 10, 1930, Dolores experienced the difficulties of the Great Depression firsthand. Her father lost his job as a coal miner because of the economic downturn. To earn money, the family picked vegetables in nearby states as migrant laborers, moving with the harvests. Strained by poverty and constant movement, Dolores's parents divorced when she was only 3 years old. She and her two brothers moved with their mother to the agricultural community of Stockton, California.

Dolores's mother taught her children that all people's voices—regardless of gender, race, or wealth—mattered. As a teen, Dolores experienced personal and immediate forms of discrimination and injustice. In high school, a teacher accused her of cheating, arguing that a Mexican American girl couldn't possibly have written the paper Dolores had submitted. Such experiences led Dolores to see that prejudice was real and that people had to rise up against it.

Unlike many women at the time—especially those from lower-income, Latino communities—Dolores attended college. She married while still a student and had two children. The marriage was brief, and when it ended, she and her daughters moved in with her mother. Dolores went back to school, earned a teaching degree, and began working in a school with a large number of migrant students. Although Dolores loved teaching, she recognized that there were factors that interfered with her students' learning. How could you expect a child whose **basic needs** weren't being met to be successful? She decided she needed to help migrant children by helping their parents.

Dolores coined the phrase, *"Si, se puede."* It means, "Yes, we can."

Today, nonviolent protests continue to be used throughout the world in response to injustice.

Middle Years: Expressing a Voice

To help launch her efforts, Dolores sought community-building partners. She first worked with the Community Service Organization (CSO) in Stockton, California. It was here that she founded the Agricultural Workers Association. Dolores gained organizing experience through voter registration drives and neighborhood improvement efforts. Through her work with CSO, Dolores met Cesar Chavez. The two recognized their mutual interest in improving the lives of farmworkers and started their own organization.

In 1962, the pair launched the National Farm Workers Association (NFWA). Strikes and **boycotts** soon became a key NFWA strategy. In 1965, the NFWA joined with Filipino grape workers to become the United Farm Workers (UFW). The organization launched a strike and boycott to inform Americans about the people who picked their grapes and the working conditions they endured. Strikers wanted the ability to unionize. This meant they would receive promised wages and contracts to assure work, along with other benefits. The grape growers responded with threats and violence. They hired **thugs** to frighten and attack strikers, and they bribed authorities.

Boycotts in History

During a boycott, people protest by refusing to purchase goods or services. The 1955–1956 Montgomery Bus Boycott is among the 20th century's most successful. Spurred by the resistance of Claudette Colvin and Rosa Parks to unjust policies, African Americans stopped using the city's bus system. Despite direct violence, including the firebombing of Martin Luther King Jr.'s house, the boycott continued. Federal courts eventually ruled bus ***segregation*** *unconstitutional. The boycott achieved its goals. It raised awareness, halted a racist practice, and set a* ***precedent*** *for future action.*

Dolores's boycott inspired an estimated 17 million people to stop buying grapes.

Throughout the 5-year strike, Dolores organized **picket lines** and made deals with growers. In April 1966, she and Cesar led strikers on a 340-mile (547 kilometers) march from Delano, California, to Sacramento, the state's capital. The media and America were now paying attention to the UFW. Dolores then planned a boycott that brought the UFW's fight from distant farm fields to America's cities. She led efforts in New York City, organizing religious, political, and peace groups to picket grocery stories and the centers where grapes were delivered. In her radio and newspaper interviews, she tried to convince the public to stop buying California table grapes.

Harsh working conditions for farm laborers included long days hunched over, no drinking water, and no medical benefits.

In 2012, Dolores was awarded the Presidential Medal of Freedom.

Her actions got the attention of other labor organizations, and the movement gained new allies. The boycott spread, and millions of families stopped buying table grapes.

In July 1970, the UFW won! Farmworkers could now unionize. Hourly wages and other benefits became standard. By then, the union had 50,000 members, the largest in the history of California. Their actions showed that peaceful organizing could lead to improvements in the quality of life for working people.

Later Years: Leaving a Legacy

Dolores continued to work on protecting farmworkers' rights. She also turned her attention to immigration, women's, and environmental justice issues. Her activism put her at great risk. In 1988, while protesting presidential candidate George H. W. Bush's stand on **pesticides**, she was severely beaten. She suffered broken ribs, a ruptured spleen, and massive blood loss.

During the 1990s, Dolores focused on getting more women and people of color elected to office. Today, she continues her work through the Dolores Huerta Foundation. She has endured arrest, beatings, imprisonment, and poverty to help underrepresented groups have a better life.

Environmental Dangers

In the early 1960s, chemicals like ***DDT*** *were used to treat crops. But evidence shows that DDT harms all living systems, including humans. Despite this, farm owners continued to spray crops, even while workers were in the fields. With Dolores's help, the grape workers' contract of 1970 included banning DDT. Two years later, the chemical was formally banned by the U.S. government.*

TIMELINE

April 10, 1930
Dolores Huerta is born in New Mexico.

May 22, 1930
Harvey Milk is born in New York.

1955
Harvey resigns from the U.S. Navy.

1962
First meeting of the NFWA.

1965
The Delano Grape Strike begins.

1970
Farmworkers and growers reach a deal in the Delano Grape Strike.

1972
Harvey moves to San Francisco, California, and opens Castro Camera.

1974
The first Castro Street Fair draws 5,000 people to the neighborhood.

1975
California passes the Agricultural Labor Relations Act, protecting the bargaining power of farmworkers.

1977
Harvey is elected city supervisor in San Francisco.

April 1978
Mayor George Moscone signs an ordinance protecting LGBT rights in San Francisco.

November 27, 1978
Harvey is assassinated at San Francisco's City Hall.

1993
Dolores becomes the first Latina in the National Women's Hall of Fame.

1998
Dolores is awarded the Eleanor Roosevelt Human Rights Award.

2012
Dolores receives the Presidential Medal of Freedom from President Obama.

2015
The U.S. Supreme Court rules that same-sex couples have the right to marry.

Research and Act

Protests, **petitions**, and boycotts are expressions of a shared voice. They were used by Harvey Milk, Dolores Huerta, and their allies to educate the public and advance their movements. Other civil rights groups used similar methods to push for social change.

Research

Investigate news sources for recent examples of protests, petitions, and boycotts. What is being protested and who is involved? When and where is it happening? How are different groups responding?

Act

How can you use protests, petitions, and boycotts to promote social justice and civil rights? Identify areas of concern in your community. Talk with peers and teachers about how you can act to create change.

Further Reading

Barghoorn, Linda. *Dolores Huerta: Advocate for Women and Workers.* St. Catharines, Ontario; New York, NY: Crabtree Publishing Company, 2017.

Brill, Marlene Targ. *Dolores Huerta Stands Strong: The Woman Who Demanded Justice.* Athens, OH: Ohio University Press, 2018.

Hollander, Barbara Gottfried. *Harvey Milk: The First Openly Gay Elected Official in the United States.* New York, NY: Rosen YA, 2018.

Pohlen, Jerome. *Gay & Lesbian History for Kids: The Century-Long Struggle for LGBT Rights.* Chicago, IL: Chicago Review Press, 2016.

Sanders, Rob. *Pride: The Story of Harvey Milk and the Rainbow Flag.* New York, NY: Random House, 2018.

GLOSSARY

assassinated (uh-SAS-uh-nate-id) murdered

basic needs (BAY-sik NEEDZ) essential needs for survival, such as food, water, shelter, and clothing

boycotts (BOI-kahtz) refusals by people to do business with others as a form of protest

DDT (DEE-DEE-TEE) short for dichloro-diphenyl-trichloroethane, a toxic chemical used to kill pests such as insects

discrimination (dis-krim-ih-NAY-shuhn) unfair behavior to others based on differences in race or gender

Great Depression (GRAYT dih-PRESH-uhn) period of global economic stress spanning from 1929 to 1939

harassment (huh-RAS-muhnt) bothering someone again and again, creating a hostile situation

homophobia (hoh-muh-FOH-bee-uh) dislike and prejudice against LGBT people

LGBT (EL-GEE-BEE-TEE) stands for lesbian, gay, bisexual, and transgender, descriptions of different sexual orientations; recently, "Q" has been added (LGBTQ), which stands for queer or questioning

ordinance (OR-duh-nuhns) law enacted by a municipality or city

pesticides (PES-tih-sidez) chemicals used to kill pests such as insects

petitions (puh-TISH-uhnz) letters signed by many people telling those in power how they feel about a certain situation

picket lines (PIK-it LINEZ) lines of people standing in a certain place, often carrying signs and shouting slogans in protest of an issue

precedent (PRES-ih-duhnt) something done, said, or written that becomes an example to be followed in the future

repatriation (ree-pay-tree-AY-shuhn) the act of sending a person back to their country of origin

segregation (seg-rih-GAY-shuhn) the practice of keeping people or groups (such as racial or ethnic) apart

sexual orientation (SEKS-yoo-uhl or-ee-uhn-TAY-shuhn) how someone identifies themselves based on who they are attracted to

stigma (STIG-muh) a mark of shame or embarrassment

stock (STAHK) a share or part of a company available to investors for purchase

thugs (THUHGZ) rough, violent people

Wall Street (WAWL STREET) the area in New York where the U.S. financial industry is located

INDEX